MANY AND GREAT
Songs of the World Church
VOLUME 1

edited & arranged by John L. Bell

design by Graham Maule

WILD GOOSE PUBLICATIONS
Iona Community
GLASGOW

First published 1990

To
our friends
throughout the world
who have given us
a bigger glimpse
of God

The Wild Goose is a Celtic symbol of the Holy Spirit.
It is the trademark of Wild Goose Publications.

Wild Goose Publications
The Publishing Division of the Iona Community
Pearce Institute, 840 Govan Road, Glasgow G51 3UT
Scotland
☎ (041) 445 − 4561

Printed in Great Britain

CONTENTS

● THE SONGS

COPYRIGHT

INTRODUCTION

It comes as a surprise to inveterate Presbyterians, Methodists, Anglicans and others to discover that their denominational hymnals are never denominational but always ecumenical.

Cardinal Newman who wrote *Praise to the Holiest in the Height* was as much a Congregationalist as John Wesley was a Catholic. This furtive kind of ecumenical sharing has been going on for centuries. And it has also crossed the national boundaries. The fine old English hymns *Now thank we all our God* and *Thine be the Glory* come, respectively from Germany and France. Their tunes are also of continental origin.

Yet this trans-denominational and international co-operation in the song of the Church has rarely, in any significant way, operated across the globe from South to North or from East to West.

This is partly because the mission routes, like the trade routes, ran in opposite directions. It was the Northern and Western nations which evangelised the Southern hemisphere and kept distant from the indigenous church life of Eastern Europe.

Accordingly, the hymnals of the 'mission' churches abounded in 19th century British favourites, irrespective of whether 'Snow had fallen, snow on snow' was an understandable Christmas allusion in Nigeria, or the 'rich man in his castle' was a sociological reality in the Pacific Islands.

The reluctance to share the song of the Southern and Eastern churches may also be attributed to a sense of religious paternalism or maternalism whereby the 'mother' churches always expect to be the donors and never the recipients. What the younger churches have to offer is presumed to be either naive or unsuited to the needs of sophisticated Westerners.

It was therefore a great surprise to us, reared in Western hymnody from childhood and in the process of writing songs of our own, to discover that material emanating from such un-Scottish places as Soweto, Buenos Aires and Budapest was not only singable but opened our eyes and challenged our assumptions about the nature of our faith.

It began when a collection of South African Songs (*Freedom is Coming*) came into our hands and almost immediately became the staple fare for enabling staid,four-square congregations to enjoy singing in harmony. They further lent themselves to use in vigils and demonstrations organised by church and secular bodies opposed to apartheid.

Later, we realised that these songs, coming from oppressed peoples, who were sometimes silenced for singing them, were actually a means of intercession. By using them we could identify with the joys and pains of Christians in other countries and offer both our concern and our solidarity to God.

Invitations to Mission Conferences, meeting people from Third World cultures at home and abroad, and the occasional encounters with people from Eastern Europe helped to swell our stock of material. In this, we have been particularly indebted to various personnel of the World Council of Churches who have made the connections essential to our work.

This first book of *Songs of the World Church* by no means exhausts our stock. It is a first volume of songs which have proven their worth in the devotional life of our own Worship Group and which have been shared by youth groups, womens' groups, church conferences and congregations large and small throughout Britain.

ABOUT THE SONGS

Many of these songs were taken down in sol-fa on the back of an envelope or whatever spare piece of paper was at hand. Others were caught by a cassette tape-recorder, hurriedly put into operation to catch a snippet in a crowded room. The minority were copied from existing manuscript.

While every effort has been taken to capture as much of the original melody and harmony as possible, this has not always been the case. Some songs came in a single line, with no indication of the underlying harmonic structure. Others came with so much harmony that it was difficult to distinguish the tune!

There are, therefore, a number of settings where only the melody comes from abroad, the four part harmony being entirely of West of Scotland devising.

The situation with regard to the words has been a bit better. By and large, we were able to get exact copies of the text. The problem arose not so much in translation as in finding English words which could both convey the sense of the original and fit into a regular metrical pattern.

Where in either words or music we have, for whatever reason, fallen short of exactness, we beg the indulgence of the users.

THEIR USE IN WORSHIP

It will be evident that not all these songs could be substituted for the third or fourth hymn at a 'normal' morning service. That is not a disadvantage; it is a gift. The worship patterns of non-European churches challenge us to break with our too convenient moulds. Using short songs, we can begin or end worship in a procession, and we may celebrate the entry of God's word or of the sacramental elements into our midst. Or we may use such songs as an aid to prayer and meditation.

In almost every case, they should not be played on an organ. This is not to disparage that instrument. It is, instead, to say that songs which arise from folk traditions and which were always intended to be sung by folk, lose their value when the voices of the people are overlayed — and sometimes overpowered — by instrumental sound.

There is nothing more excruciating than hearing a South African freedom song, which relies on syncopation and body rhythm, being forced into musical corsets by an organ fundamentalist who refuses to believe that anything can be sung in church unless he or she is at the console. Such musicians need liberated.

IN CONCLUSION

These songs came to us at an important time in world affairs. The entrenchment of Eastern European nations, the intransigence of white South African governments, the brutal dictatorships of Central and Southern America are all in the melting pot. And we believe that God has put them there in response to the prayer, protest and song of his people which has risen from hope and suffering.

It is because we believe that as Western Europeans we are called on at this time in history to learn from the experience of those we previously colonised, that we have not included in this collection songs from the former imperial powers. In future books we will include some such. But this collection is offered as a celebration of the work of God and the witness of God's people whose worship has made headline news in heaven.

John Bell
Wild Goose Worship Group
Pentecost 1990

A companion cassette which includes all songs in this collection is available. Entitled *Many and Great*, it was recorded by the Wild Goose Worship Group and may be purchased from retailers or Wild Goose Publications.

SONGS OF THE WORLD CHURCH

GLORIA

ARGENTINA

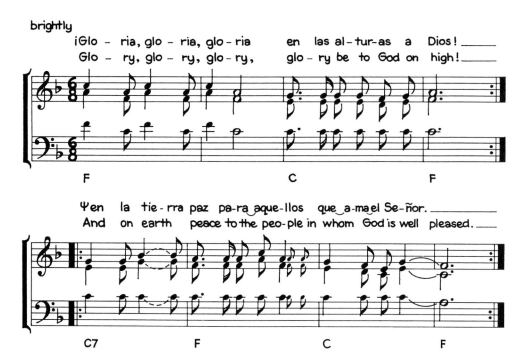

brightly

¡Glo – ria, glo – ria, glo – ria   en las al – tur-as   a   Dios! ____
Glo – ry, glo – ry, glo – ry,   glo – ry be to God on high! ____

F   C   F

Ψ en   la tie – rra paz pa-ra aque-llos que a-ma el Se – ñor. ____
And   on earth   peace to the peo-ple in whom God is well pleased. ____

C7   F   C   F

Gloria, gloria, gloria
en las alturas a Dios!
Y en la tierra paz para aquellos
que ama el Senor.

Glory, glory, glory,
glory be to God on high!
And on earth peace to the people
in whom God is well pleased.

The *Cueca* is a national dance of Chile, Bolivia and Argentina, where, in a central square in Buenos Aires, it is sometimes danced by women alone whose husbands have 'disappeared'.

The juxtaposition of 3/4 and 6/8 rhythms makes for a feeling of ambiguity in the music which is reflected in the text, 'peace to the people in whom God is well pleased.' Who are these people — the powerful or the powerless?

This Gloria, set to the *Cueca* rhythm, was originally composed for a nativity play and had, as its only percussive accompaniment, the panderita. It should be sung with joy and lightness.

Pablo Sosa, the composer, is an Argentinian Methodist minister and one of the foremost South American authorities on religious music in the folkloristic tradition.

Words : traditional liturgical text.
Music : © 1990 Pablo Sosa.

SANTO

ARGENTINA

quietly and steadily

San - to, san - to, san-to, mi cor - a - zon te a-do - ra! Mi
Ho - ly, ho - ly, ho - ly, my heart, my heart a-dores you! My

C   G7   Am   F   C7   C

cor - a - zon te sa - be de-cir: san-to e-res Se - ñor. _____
heart is glad to say the words: you are ho - ly, Lord. _____

F   G7   C   Am   F   C7   C

Santo, santo, santo,
mi corazon te adora!
Mi corazon te sabe decir:
santo eres Senor.

Holy, holy, holy,
my heart, my heart adores you !
My heart is glad to say the words:
you are holy, Lord.

The music which accompanies the words of the *Sanctus* very often indicates something about the theology of the composer as well as the context for which it was written. A *Sanctus* by Palestrina, for example, may point to a God who is remote and enthroned in unattainable bliss, to be sung in a liturgy attended by people of social and ecclesiastical standing and sophistication.

This *Sanctus* comes from a very different background. It is a heartfelt love song of people who know what suffering means and who sense their solidarity with Christ who suffers with them.

It should be sung slowly but steadily.

Words :   variation on traditional liturgical text.
Music :   composer of melody unknown;
        arrangement © 1990 Iona Community
        based on two-part version as taught by Pablo Sosa.

SENHOR,
TEMPIEDADE DÉ NOS

BRAZIL

Senhor, tempiedade de nos.
Cristo, tempiedade de nos.
Senhor, tempiedade de nos.

Lord our God, have mercy on us.
Jesus Christ, have mercy on us.
Lord our God, have mercy on us.

This is a very beautiful setting of the *Kyrie* which shows harmonic intensity not normally associated with Central and Southern America.

It should be sung in a slow and stately fashion, preferably in four parts. The English translation is an enlargement on the Portuguese text to suit the music.

Jaci Maraschin, the composer, is an Anglican theologian working in Sao Paulo. He has written a wide range of liturgical music, often drawing on indigenous rhythmic patterns.

Words : traditional liturgical text.
Music : © 1990 Jaci Maraschin.

HE CAME DOWN

CAMEROONS

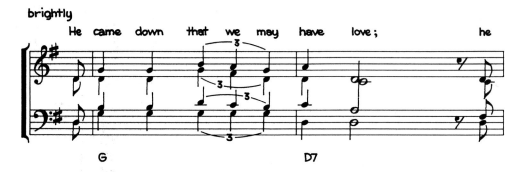

love
peace
joy.
faith.
hope.

1. He came down that we may have love;
    he came down that we may have love;
    he came down that we may have love,
        hallelujah for evermore.
        (repeat verse)

2. He came down that we may have peace;
    he came down that we may have peace;
    he came down that we may have peace,
        hallelujah for evermore.
        (repeat verse)

3. He came down that we may have joy;
    he came down that we may have joy;
    he came down that we may have joy,
        hallelujah for evermore.
        (repeat verse)

This song was experienced by us at an international conference in Germany in 1986, when a group of presbyterians from the Cameroons broke into a song and dance. They moved in a circle, anti-clockwise, using their hands to beckon Christ, as it were, from heaven to earth.

The song is sung at a moderate speed and at the end of the first singing of each verse, the cantor calls, "Why did he come?" to encourage the company to repeat what they have sung.

Words : traditional.
Music : origin unknown;
         arrangement transcribed from voices 1986 (JLB).

STAND FIRM

CAMEROONS

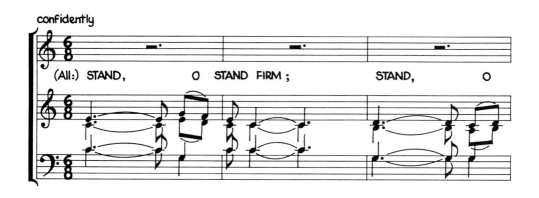

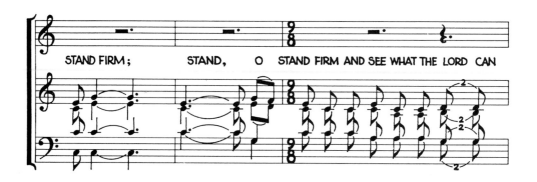

All :   **Stand, O stand firm;**
stand, O stand firm;
stand, O stand firm
and see what the Lord can do.

Cantor :   **O my sisters, stand very firm!**

All :   **Stand, O stand firm;**
stand, O stand firm;
stand, O stand firm
and see what the Lord can do.

Cantor :   *(other verses ad lib)*

One evening at the World Conference on Mission and Evangelism in San Antonio, Texas, (May 1989), a woman from the Cameroons stood up in an informal gathering, to sing this song.

The impression given was that any group of people or any individual may be called upon by name in the course of the singing, at the cantor's discretion. This would be in keeping with a similar practice seen in another context where a Cameroonian cantor engaged unsuspecting people to attend to the Lord's business.

The song should be sung with deliberation, the volume rising and falling depending on who is being called to stand firm.

Words : traditional.
Music : origin unknown;
arrangement © 1990 Iona Community.

HALLE, HALLE, HALLE

CARIBBEAN

lively tempo

Halle, halle, halle — lujah!
Halle, halle, halle — lujah!
Halle, halle, halle — lujah!
Hallelujah, hallelujah!

This is a very lively and enjoyable *Hallelujah*, suitable for a recessional or as a song during which people may move, for whatever purpose, in the sanctuary. It may also be used after the reading of the scriptures.

The four part setting is not native to the Caribbean. Only the anonymous melody line appeared in the source document.

Words : traditional liturgical text.
Music : origin unknown;
arrangement © 1990 Iona Community.

MAY GOD DRAW NEAR

CZECHOSLOVAKIA

moderato

May God draw near when the hour of trou-ble strikes; ___ may

Ja - cob's God be your strength and shield; _____

out of the sanc-tu-ary, out of his home, may

God pro - vide in your time of need. ___

last time

1. May God draw near when the hour of trouble strikes;
   may Jacob's God be your strength and shield;
   out of the sanctuary, out of his home,
   may God provide in your time of need.

2. May God remember the sacrifice you make
   and take delight in the gifts you bring.
   May God respond to your heart's deep desire
   and grant fulfilment to all your plans.

3. With every blessing our mouths will shout for joy
   to celebrate what the Lord has done;
   and ever after, when God shows you favour,
   in every triumph we'll trace his love.

4. O now I know that the Lord is God indeed
   and grants success to his chosen one.
   From highest heaven God answers my call
   and brings me victory with his right hand.

5. Some trust in weapons and some in skills of war,
   but all we have is our faith in God.
   They that are mighty shall stumble and fall
   but we will rise and shall overcome.

We are indebted to the Revs. Tomas and Daniella Bisek for the inclusion of two Czech hymns in this collection. Tomas, a signator of Charter 77, was forced to live in exile in Scotland where he became a minister of the Church of Scotland.

This is a psalm setting from the hymnbook of the Evangelical Church of the Czech Brethren.

The tune, by the contemporary composer Zdenek Cep, is an example of the beauty of Eastern European melodic writing which combines modernity of style with an evident sympathy for ethnic musical traditions.

Words : Psalm 20;
            paraphrase © 1990 Iona Community.
Music :   © 1990 Zdenek Cep.

THE LORD IS MY LIGHT

CZECHOSLOVAKIA

1. The Lord is my light,
   my light and my salvation.
   With God protecting me from every danger,
   whom shall I fear?

2. Should evil powers advance,
   should armies try to kill,
   let them surround me and let them attack me,
   I'll still trust God.

3. One thing I ask the Lord.
   This only I desire:
   always in worship to gaze at God's goodness
   and seek his aid.

4. Preserved by God from harm,
   secure in him alone,
   I will rejoice in the face of affliction
   and sing God's song.

The song comes from the *Evangelicky Zpelsnik* hymnbook of the Evangelical Church of the Czech Brethren. It is a setting of the words of Psalm 27 to a traditional Czech post-reformation tune.

When we sing the words of this song, remembering the recent history of the occupation of Czechoslovakia, we get an insight into the power of the psalms as hymns of protest, as relevant to contemporary tyrannical regimes as those of the Ancient Near East.

Words : Psalm 27 vs 1 − 6;
         paraphrase © 1990 Iona Community.
Music : Czech c. 17th hymn tune.

KYRIE ELEISON

GHANA

Kyrie eleison.

Lord, have mercy.

This *Kyrie* was composed in 1987 by Dinah Reindorf, a Nigerian who formerly conducted the Nigerian National Orchestra.

Dinah had been at a W.C.C. consultation on music, during which the participants took part in a 'Passion Walk' — a blindfold experience of walking in Christ's footsteps to the cross.

The impact was so great on her that this very beautiful and sonorous *Kyrie* came to her mind.

The *Kyrie* stands perfectly well on its own as a unison melody.
The four part arrangement is of Scottish origin.

Words : traditional liturgical text.
Music : melody © 1987 Dinah Reindorf;
   arrangement © 1990 Iona Community.

JESUS CHRIST,
OUR LIVING LORD

HUNGARY

moderato

Je-sus Christ, our liv – ing Lord, we be-lieve you

keep your word. What – ev – er may be-fall us,

stretch or stall us, we'll trust your voice to call us.

1. Jesus Christ, our living Lord,
   we believe you keep your word.
   Whatever may befall us,
   stretch or stall us,
   we'll trust your voice to call us.

2. In the humblest things we do,
   we'll account ourselves to you,
   making your love our measure,
   truth and treasure;
   your will our joy and pleasure.

3. Food enough that all may feed,
   grace enough for each one's need:
   even as we praise you, singing,
   you come bringing
   gifts at the day's beginning.

4. Lord in all we do today,
   let our lives prepare your way.
   May peace and love befriend us
   and defend us
   where you require and send us.

This song comes from the *Okumenicus Enekeskonyu*, a hymnbook of 80 items published by the Hungarian Ecumenical Council of Churches in 1981. The collection includes hymns from the various traditions represented in the Council and also some new compositions, of which this is one.

The words — of which this setting is very much a paraphrase, due to the complexities of rhyming — was written by Erzsebet Turmezei, a well known Hungarian poet. The music is by Sandor Szokolay, a Lutheran and Professor of Composition at the Liszt Ferenc Academy of Music in Budapest. As with other Hungarian composers, Szokolay in his operas, oratorios, cantatas etc. draws heavily on the rich seams of ethnic folk music.

Words: © 1979 Erzsebet Turmezei;
translated by Erzsebet Abraham;
paraphrased 1990 (JLB).

Music: © 1981 Szokolay Sandor.

YESUVE SARANAM

INDIA

steadily

(Cantor:) Ye – su – ve sa – ra – nam, sa – ra – nam Ye – su – ve.

(All:) YE – SU – VE SA – RA – NAM, SA – RA – NAM YE – SU – VE.

(Cantor:) Ye – su – ve sa – ra – nam, sa – ra – nam Ye – su – ve.

(All:) YE – SU – VE SA – RA – NAM, SA – RA – NAM YE – SU – VE.

(Cantor:) Ye – su – ve sa – ra – nam, sa – ra – nam Ye – su – ve.

(All:) YE – SU – VE SA – RA – NAM, SA – RA – NAM YE – SU – VE.

(Cantor:) Ye – su – ve sa – ra – nam, sa – ra – nam Ye – su – ve.

(All:) YE – SU – VE SA – RA – NAM, SA – RA – NAM YE – SU – VE.

Yesuve saranam, saranam Yesuve.

Jesus, I surrender.

The Church in North and South India has recently been developing forms of worship and song which relate more to the indigenous cultural roots of the people than to Western Europe.

Yesuve Saranam is an example of this. It is a song which may be used to call people to worship or to prepare for worship.

Each of the four sections is sung first by the cantor and then repeated by everyone. It has a bright tempo, slowing down a little in the final section at the last singing.

The Indian minister who introduced us to this song, clapped his hands in time to the music, two claps per bar. On the first clap, the back of his right hand met the palm of his left; on the second, the palm of the right met the palm of the left. This was more a means of keeping time than making a loud percussive sound.

Words : traditional.
Music : origin unknown;
transcribed 1987 (JLB).

LET THE WORLD IN CONCERT SING

MALAWI

confidently with no pause between verses

34

1. <u>Let the world</u> in concert <u>sing</u>
   <u>praises to our</u> glorious <u>King.</u>
   ALLELUIA, ALLELUIA TO OUR KING.

2. Of his <u>power and glory tell:</u>
   All his <u>work he does so well.</u>

3. Come, be<u>hold what he has done:</u>
   Deeds of <u>wonder every one.</u>

4. O ye <u>fearful ones draw near.</u>
   Praise the <u>God who holds you dear.</u>

5. Let us <u>now in concert sing</u>
   <u>praises to our</u> glorious <u>King.</u>

This is an English setting of a Malawian hymn based on Psalm 100. The version was originally published in a book entitled *Tunes of Nyasaland.*

The song should be sung with a strong rhythmic feeling, at least one foot keeping time on the floor, and there should be no break between verses.

The harmony setting originated in Scotland, not Malawi, and to facilitate its use, the following should be observed:

   a)   words underlined are the only words sung by the tenors.

   b)   basses, with the exception of verse 1, sing only the last three syllables of lines 1 & 2 in each verse.

Words :   © 1968 Tom Colvin.
Music :   traditional;
            arrangement © 1990 Iona Community.

SARA SHRISTE

NEPAL

gently

Sa-ra shri-ste ko ma-lik ta-paiy-lay; sa-ra shri-ste ko
You are au-thor and Lord of cre-a-tion; you are ma-ker of

Ah. _____ Ah. _____

A   F#m/A   E   A

ra-jah ta-paiy-lay. Ham-bro rhe-day s'a-me-ta-le
life and of liv-ing. And from deep in our hearts.

Ah. _____

A7   D   Bm   Bm7   E7

ad-har pra-nam; s'ad-aiy-bahns ta-paiy-ko gun-gan. ___
won-der and love in-spire our wor-ship and praise. ___

A   E   Bm7   E7   A

36

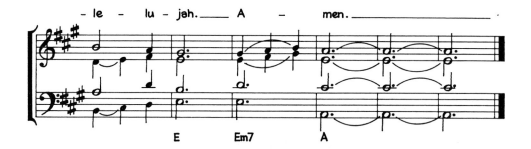

Sara shriste ko malik tapaiylay;
sara shriste ko rajah tapaiylay.
Hambro rheday s'ametale adhar pranam;
s'adaiybahns tapaiyko gungan.

    Hallelujah.   Hallelujah.
    Hallelujah.   Hallelujah.
    Hallelujah.   Hallelujah.
    Hallelujah.   Amen.

You are author and Lord of creation;
you are maker of life and of living.
And from deep in our hearts, wonder and love
inspire our worship and praise.

    Hallelujah.   Hallelujah.
    Hallelujah.   Hallelujah.
    Hallelujah.   Hallelujah.
    Hallelujah.   Amen.

This song comes from a part of Nepal where people face both poverty and the possibility of persecution for being Christian. Despite its obvious European origins, it is a song of the poor who have written the words and adapted the melody. (The leap of a 7th at the fifth Hallelujah is not a Western feature.)

The song was taught us by a Philippino working in a Danish mission. The translation of the words is not literal.

Words : origin unknown.
Music : melody probably of European origin;
        song taught by Elisabeth Padillo-Oleson;
        arrangement © 1990 Iona Community.

IMELA

NIGERIA

brightly

Imela, imela, imela, Okaka.
Imela, Chineke. Imela Ony'oma.

Thank you, great God.
Thank you because you are good.

This song of gratitude in Ibo was taught by a Nigerian journalist covering events at the San Antonio World Mission and Evangelism Conference.

She sang the melody line only from which the harmony suggested itself.

Words : traditional.
Music : © 1990 Christ Church Gospel Band, Uwani-Engu;
as taught by Mrs Unoaku Ekwegbalu;
arrangement © 1990 Iona Community.

WA WA WA EMIMIMO

NIGERIA

Wa wa wa Emimimo.
Wa wa wa Alagbara.
Wao, wao, wao.

Come, O Holy Spirit, come.
Come, Almighty Spirit, come.
Come, come, come.

The song is a beautiful invocation of the Holy Spirit in the Yoruba language. It is sung throughout Central Africa and the context in which it is used determines its speed.

At a lively gathering, it may be sung quickly and excitedly, with the worshippers raising their hands and beckoning the Spirit to come down. At other times it may be sung quietly and meditatively.

Words : traditional.
Music : as taught by Samuel Solanke;
transcription and paraphrase © 1990 I-to-Loh.

BLESSED BE GOD

PHILIPPINES

1. Blessed be God, blessed be God forever,
   who in time and eternity lives,
   God the Lord who loves justice and mercy
   and who heals and forgives those who fall.

2. God will bandage the wounds of the broken,
   and pay heed to each body and soul;
   God has asked humankind not to fear
   but believe that the kingdom's at hand.

3. Come, O Lord, come and save the oppressed,
   lift the poor from the doors of despair;
   put a song in the hearts of your people,
   those whose hope and whose trust is in you.

The tune *Dandasoy* is originally set to a love song which came from the little village of Payao on the island of Negros, Western Visayas. The composer is unknown.

The words of this song were written by Dr. Salvador T. Martinez, a minister of the United Church of Christ in the Philippines. He is currently the executive secretary for Theological Concerns of the Christian Conference of Asia. The song was written in Chiang Mai, Thailand in 1989.

Words : © 1989 Salvador T. Martinez;
           adapted (JLB).
Music : traditional;
           arrangement © 1990 Iona Community.

AMEN. ALLELUIA !

SOUTH AFRICA.

Amen. Alleluia !

This was probably a wedding song in origin.

George Mxadana relates how he had heard it used as a dispersal song in the independent churches which were set up when black people were transported to the 'homelands.'

Not having church buildings, worship was frequently held in the open air, sometimes under the shade of trees. At the end of worship, as people went their own way, they might leave singing this song and sing their own part until out of earshot of the others.

It should be sung with vigour but not too quickly.

Words :   traditional liturgical text.
Music :   traditional;
         transcribed from the singing of George Mxadana
         and Sr. Monica Mothile 1989 (JLB).

AMEN SIAKUDUMISA

SOUTH AFRICA

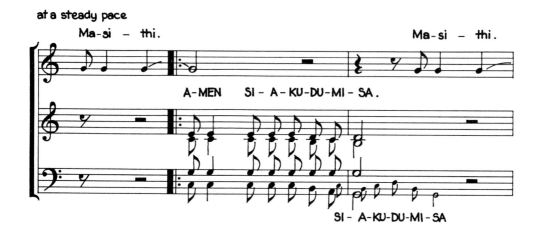

Amen siakudumisa !
Amen siakudumisa !
Amen bawo. Amen bawo.
Amen siakudumisa !

Amen. Praise the name of the Lord !

George Mxadana, a native of Soweto and a prominent South African choral conductor, tells of how this song was sung at the enthronement of Desmond Tutu as Archbishop of Capetown. When the song, from the Independent Church tradition, was taken up by the congregation, Tutu began to move in time to the music. This, for black South Africans, was a great sign that their music and culture was being recognised as integral to the worship of God.

The cantor sings 'Masithi' as an encouragement for the congregation and the basses can split their line as appropriate. Sing at a steady pace.

Words :   traditional.
Music :   attributed to S.C. Molefe;
           as taught by George Mxadana.

NDINGEN' ENDUMISWENI

SOUTH AFRICA

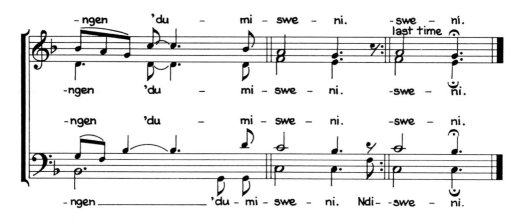

Ndingen' endumisweni.

Lord, let me enter your kingdom.

More than any other song in this collection, this item may err from the original.

It was taught by a very excited George Mxadana, singing into a small cassette recorder and — or so it seems — singing the four parts at one time.

It has to be said that many songs from South Africa do not have a 'definitive' version. The harmony and the words may vary from region to region. It is to be hoped that this version is not too far from the norm. It is certainly very enjoyable to sing.

Words :   traditional.
Music :   traditional;
                reconstructed from fragments 1989 (JLB).

MAYENZIWE

SOUTH AFRICA

not too quickly

Mayenziwe 'ntando yakho.

Your will be done on earth, O Lord.

This is a very straightforward but joyful song of affirmation. It can be sung in English, but conveys much more if the original language (Xhosa) is used.

It may be sung at the conclusion of prayers or preaching or as a recessional.

Words :   from the Lord's Prayer.
Music :   traditional;
           as taught by George Mxadana;
           transcribed 1988 (JLB).

MANY AND GREAT

U.S.A. (NATIVE TRADITION)

mysteriously

Man - y and great, ___ O God, are your works, ___ Mak - er of

earth and sky; _____ your hands have set __ the heav - ens with

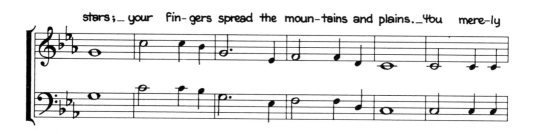

stars; __ your fin - gers spread the moun - tains and plains. __ You mere-ly

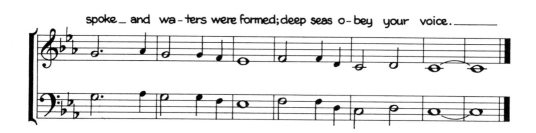

spoke __ and wa - ters were formed; deep seas o - bey your voice. _____

1. Many and great, O God, are your works,
   Maker of earth and sky;
   your hands have set the heavens with stars;
   your fingers spread the mountains and plains.
   You merely spoke and waters were formed;
   deep seas obey your voice.

2. Grant us communion with you, our God,
   though you transcend the stars.
   Come close to us and stay by our side:
   with you are found the true gifts that last.
   Bless us with life which never shall end,
   eternal life with you.

This very plaintive melody could hardly come from anything other than an American Indian community. It is both serene and haunting. The words, which were published in the *1916 Dakota Indian Hymnal* speak of the distinctive relationship between the earth and humanity which is expressed in other native works such as *The Testimony of Chief Seattle*.

The song should be sung gently at a steady pace.

Words :   *Dakota Indian Hymnal ;*
            paraphrased by Philip Frazier (1892–1964);
            © 1916 Walton Music.
Music :   traditional.

AGIOS O THEOS

U.S.S.R.

steadily

A – gi – os o The – os, a – gi – os is – chi – ros,

a – gi – os a – tha – na – tos, e – le – i – son i – mas._____

Agios o Theos,
agios ischiros,
agios athanatos,
eleison imas.

Holy God,
holy and mighty,
holy and immortal,
have mercy on us.

This Russian Orthodox liturgical song uses Greek words for a text commonly referred to as the *Trisagion*.

In comparison to the Argentinian *Santo*, it is more formal and has a greater sense of mystery. It should be sung slowly but firmly.

Words :   traditional.
Music :   from the Russian Orthodox tradition.

KYRIE ELEISON

U.S.S.R.

slowly

Ky - ri-e e - lei - son. Ky - ri-e e - lei - son.

Ky - ri-e e - le — i - son.

slowly

Ky — ri-e e - lei - son. Ky - ri-e e - lei - son.

Ky — ri-e e - lei — son.

Kyrie eleison.

Lord, have mercy.

This very simple and popular *Kyrie* was one of the first items of music from the Russian Orthodox liturgy to make its way into world-wide usage.

In a formal eucharistic liturgy, it may be used at the appropriate place for the *Kyrie*. In less formal settings, it may sung as a response during prayers or, repeatedly, as a means of meditation.

Words : traditional.
Music : from the Russian Orthodox tradition.

YOUR KINGDOM COME, O LORD

U.S.S.R.

Your kingdom come, O Lord.

The melody to this text from the Lord's Prayer was written by Professor Zabolotski, for some time a staff member of the World Council of Churches in Geneva, for the 1980 Conference for World Mission and Unity at Melbourne.

In *The International Review of Mission*, June 1980, he described his composition thus:

'The melody shows the growth of a demand in connection to the kingdom of God. In the first part, you can feel the indefinite and unsure question of an unbalanced humanity; the answer to it can be seen in the second part, as the expression of hope, but still in the form of a question. The third part expresses the demanding cry from the depth of human unhappiness, poverty, suffering and oppression, a cry to Christ high in his heavenly kingdom: the striving for the kingdom! The fourth part is a definite underlined response. It is the justification of hope: "Yes, the kingdom is coming indeed."

'We should perform the melody starting very softly, with the feeling of piety and gradually expanding the expressiveness of the idea itself. The special accent must be on the last part – "Your kingdom come, O Lord." '

Words :   from the Lord's Prayer.
Music :   melody © 1980 Prof. Nicolai Zabolotski;
            arrangement © 1990 Iona Community.

JESU TAWA PANO

ZIMBABWE

Jesu tawa pano;
Jesu tawa pano;
Jesu tawa pano;
tawa pano mu zita renyu.

Jesus, we are here;
Jesus, we are here;
Jesus, we are here;
we are here for you.

This is an original composition in Shona by Patrick Matsikenyiri, a leading figure in African church music, who combines being headmaster of a primary school with leading and teaching songs for worship all over the world.

The song should be sung joyfully and can be accompanied with with maracas or other percussive instruments.

This is one of over 80 songs which Patrick has composed and which he keeps (in four or more parts) in his head. After I transcribed this song, I mentioned that there seemed to be a clash in the harmony in bar 5, where the tenor sings a major 7th above the bass.

Patrick laughed and said, 'My dear John, if you knew the history of our country, you would know that we have had so many clashes that a little difficulty in the harmony will cause us no problems.'

ACKNOWLEDGEMENTS

Below are listed the copyright holders of various items in this collection. Permission to reproduce must be obtained from them whenever appropriate. Translation of words copyright the Iona Community may be freely reproduced for one-off non commercial purposes as long as appropriate acknowledgement is made.

In thanking the copyright holders for granting permission for words and music to be printed, we also wish to record our very deep gratitude to people throughout the world who have, by their effort and encouragement, helped this book to move from a hope to a reality. In particular we are indebted to:

Jean Stromberg & Terry MacArthur   —   World Council of Churches
Erzsebet Abraham   —   Hungary
Daniella & Tomas Bisek   —   Czechoslovakia/Scotland
Unoaku Ekwegbalu   —   Nigeria
Per Harling   —   Sweden
I-to-Loh   —   Philippines
Patrick Matsikenyiri   —   Zimbabwe
George Mxadana   —   South Africa
Elizabeth Padillo-Oleson   —   Nepal
Pablo Sosa   —   Argentina
Milos Vesin   —   Czechoslovakia
The Resident Group and particularly the musicians of Iona Abbey.
Members of the Wild Goose Worship Group.
Maggie Simpson, our secretary.
Michael Lee, Publications Manager.

COPYRIGHT HOLDERS

ARGENTINA
Gloria — Pablo Sosa, Buenos Aires, Argentina.
Santo — Origin unknown.

BRAZIL
Senhor tempiedade de nos — Jaci C. Maraschin, Sao Paulo, Brazil.

CAMEROONS
He came down — Origin unknown.
Stand firm — Origin unknown.

CARIBBEAN
Halle, halle, halle — Origin unknown.

CZECHOSLOVAKIA
May God draw near — Synodni Ruda, Jungmannoba 9, Prague 1, Czechoslovakia.
The Lord is my light — Synodni Ruda, Jungmannoba 9, Prague 1, Czechoslovakia.

GHANA
Kyrie Eleison — Dinah Reindorf, Accra, Ghana.

HUNGARY
Jesus Christ, our living Lord — Original words : Erzsebet Turmezei. Music : Szokolay Sandor, Budapest, Hungary.

INDIA
Yesuve Saranam — Origin unknown.

MALAWI
Let the world in concert sing — Hope Publishing Company, Carol Stream, Illinois, U.S.A.

NEPAL
Sara shriste — Samdan Publishers, Kathmandu, Nepal.

NIGERIA
Imela — Christ Church Gospel Band, Box 434, Uwani-Enugu, Anambra State, Nigeria.
Wa wa wa Emimimo — Origin unknown.

PHILIPPINES
Blessed be God — Original words : Salvador T. Martinez, Thailand.

SOUTH AFRICA
Amen. Alleluia ! — Origin unknown.
Amen siakudumisa — Origin unknown.
Ndingen' endumisweni — Origin unknown.
Mayenziwe — Origin unknown.

U.S.A.
Many and great — Walton Music, New York, U.S.A.

U.S.S.R.
Agios o Theos — Origin unknown.
Kyrie Eleison — Origin unknown.
Your Kingdom come — Nikolai A. Zabolotski , Geneva, Switzerland.

ZIMBABWE
Jesu tawa pano — Patrick Matsikenyiri, Cashel, Zimbabwe.

COPYRIGHT

ALPHABETICAL INDEX OF FIRST LINES

CURRENT PUBLICATIONS OF THE IONA COMMUNITY

THE WHOLE EARTH SHALL CRY GLORY	Paperback ISBN 0 947988 00 9
THE WHOLE EARTH SHALL CRY GLORY	Hardback ISBN 0 947988 04 1
Iona prayers by Rev. George F. MacLeod	
THE IONA COMMUNITY WORSHIP BOOK	ISBN 0 947988 28 9
Iona Community	
THE CORACLE – REBUILDING THE COMMON LIFE	ISBN 0 947988 25 4
Jubilee reprint of Foundation Documents of the Iona Community	
PEACE AND ADVENTURE	ISBN 0 9501351 6 X
Ellen Murray	
90 RECIPES FROM THE IONA COMMUNITY	ISBN 0 947988 17 3
Sue Pattison	
RE-INVENTING THEOLOGY	ISBN 0 947988 29 7
Ian M. Fraser	
MEANING THE LORD'S PRAYER	ISBN 0 947988 30 0
George T. H. Reid	
PARABLES AND PATTER	ISBN 0 947988 33 5
Erik Cramb	
HEAVEN SHALL NOT WAIT (Wild Goose Songs Volume 1)	ISBN 0 947988 23 8
John Bell & Graham Maule	
WILD GOOSE SONGS – VOLUME 2	ISBN 0 947988 27 0
John Bell & Graham Maule	
LOVE FROM BELOW (Wild Goose Songs Volume 3)	ISBN 0 947988 34 3
John Bell & Graham Maule	
A TOUCHING PLACE	Cassette No.IC/WGP/004
Wild Goose Worship Group	
CLOTH FOR THE CRADLE	Cassette No.IC/WGP/007
Wild Goose Worship Group	
LOVE FROM BELOW	Cassette No.IC/WGP/008
Wild Goose Worship Group	
FOLLY AND LOVE	Cassette No.IC/WGP/005
Iona Abbey	
FREEDOM IS COMING	Cassette No.IC/WGP/006
FREEDOM IS COMING	ISBN 91 86788 15 7
Utryck	
MANY AND GREAT (World Church Songs - Volume 1)	ISBN 0 947988 40 8
John Bell & Graham Maule	
MANY AND GREAT	Cassette IC/WGP/009
Wild Goose Worship Group	
WILD GOOSE PRINTS No.1	ISBN 0 947988 06 8
John Bell & Graham Maule	
WILD GOOSE PRINTS No.2	ISBN 0 947988 10 6
John Bell & Graham Maule	
WILD GOOSE PRINTS No.3	ISBN 0 947988 24 6
John Bell & Graham Maule	
WILD GOOSE PRINTS No.4	ISBN 0 947988 35 1
John Bell & Graham Maule	
WILD GOOSE PRINTS No. 5	ISBN 0 947988 41 6
John Bell & Graham Maule	
EH . . . JESUS . . . YES, PETER . . . ? Book 1	ISBN 0 947988 20 3
John Bell & Graham Maule	
EH . . . JESUS . . . YES, PETER . . .? Book 2	ISBN 0 947988 31 9
John Bell & Graham Maule	
WHAT IS THE IONA COMMUNITY?	ISBN 0 947988 07 6
Iona Community	
CO-OPERATION VERSUS EXPLOITATION	ISBN 0 947988 22 X
Walter Fyfe	
COLUMBA	ISBN 0 947988 11 4
Mitchell Bunting	
FEEL IT – Detached Youth Work In Action	ISBN 0 947988 32 7
Cilla McKenna	
PRAISING A MYSTERY	ISBN 0 947988 36 X
Brian Wren	
BRING MANY NAMES	ISBN 0 947988 37 8
Brian Wren	